the **best** *in*

sportswear

design

the *best* in
sportswear
design

Joy McKenzie

Foreword by Sally Gunnell

◀ **Converse Activewear:** cycle top and
shorts in jersey and cotton twill from the
Extreme Sports Collection with 'Go faster'
stripes, cut n' sew panelling, bright colour
blocks and contast stitching.

Acknowledgements

I would like to thank my family and friends, with special thanks to those most directly involved in the production of this publication without whose support it would not have been possible. To Richard Reynolds, Executive Editor; Martina Stansbie, Editor and Julie Ambrose, former secretary for BT Batsford Ltd; Sally Gunnell, Olympic Champion; Peter G. Yarranton, chairman of the Sports Council; Mark McCormack, international sports promoter; John Hammond and Monica Fernandez of R.D. Franks Ltd; Roger Coleman, author and founder of London Innovation; Eammon McCabe, the only photographer to have won the 'Sports Photographer of the Year Award' three times; Dr Howard Payne, lecturer in Biomechanics at the London School of Sport and Exercise Sciences; Dominic Hilton-Foster, press officer at Harrods; The London College of Fashion Library; the National Art Library; The British Retail Consortium; The British Fashion Council; Caroline Carr at The Women's Sport Foundation; Helen Bonser at the British Sports and Allied Industries Federation and, finally, The British Sports Council.

Dedication

This book is dedicated to my parents Mitchell and Monica McKenzie,

Printed in China

for the Publisher

B.T. Batsford Ltd

583 Fulham Road

London SW6 5BY

ISBN 0 7134 8027 0

A CIP catalogue record for this book is available from the British Library.

contents

Sally Gunnell

Foreword

Sally Gunnell

The unveiling of new styling and fabrics is something I look forward to every season. State-of-the-art designs and fabric help to give me that vital edge in performance and the confidence to be a winner. In The Best in Sportswear Design you'll discover fashion that makes a difference - both on and off the track.

Introduction

The emergence of a sporting culture over the last 150 years has seen the acceptance of physically fit athletic men and women as cultural and aesthetic ideals. The perfect body has become an object of desire and, consequently, most sports clothing today is designed not only to be technically efficient and increase a competitor's effectiveness but also to reveal the body beneath it.

In 1982 actress Jane Fonda released her first aerobic exercise video tape, bringing exercise to a whole new segment of the population: full-time homemakers and mothers. Magazines and the cosmetics industry helped to reinforce the belief in health, exercise and youth. As aerobics increased in popularity, loosely-fitting clothes or the rather ugly sensible black nylon leotard with long sleeves were gradually replaced by wrestler leotards worn over cropped tops or thong-style briefs with high-cut legs. These garments were made in fabrics that both clung to the body and stretched and so allowed an increased range of movement.

Even if we cannot achieve the perfect body, we continue to subscribe to the belief in health and fitness by appropriating sports apparel for work, school and leisure: witness the dominance of the running shoe. With the explosion of the fitness craze in the 1970s it is not surprising that the fashion industry adopted both the fabric technology and the garments and soon the catwalks of Paris and Milan had models in designer versions of spandex cycle shorts and running shoes. Clothing that was once worn exclusively by athletes or for fitness and sports activities – running shoes, muscle shirts, tank tops, sweatshirts and even soccer shirts complete with sponsor's logo and player's name – are all now worn outside the gym and off the sports field. In the 1980s, Hip Hop culture – its language, music, dance and art – broke into the mainstream and consequently Hip Hop fashion, particularly the hooded tracksuit, became the fashion of popular youth culture, legitimizing sports apparel brands like Puma and adidas as authentic street clothing.

◀ **Speedo:** 'Explosion Olympic' performance swimsuit.

Gender has played an important role in the shaping of our sporting experience and in the development of sports clothing. A widespread assumption of female fraility put up barriers against women taking part in some (if not all) sports until the late nineteenth century. While this myth has now been shattered, many are, nevertheless, uneasy about the idea of aggressive competitive sportswomen like Cindy Martin (who boxed ten rounds on the same card as Mike Tyson and Frank Bruno) and Jill Matthews (the first female Golden Gloves boxing champion). Thousands of women across Europe and the United States are taking up boxing both professionally and as aerobic exercise. While Everlast, the 80-year-old New York brand of authentic boxing gear, has responded to the new interest in the sport by licensing its name to manufacturers of women's wear and accessories (and consequently increasing its market share by 50 per cent) many still find the idea of women participating in an aggressive and potentially dangerous contact sport too much to bear.

This reaction does, however, remind us of the continuing presence of traditional sex-role stereotyping and also helps to explain why women wearing bloomers and riding bicycles in the 1890s caused such an outrage. In the late nineteenth century, the idea of a woman wearing pants in part undermined the concept that clothing defined and distinguished the sexes. Also related to questions of dress was whether it was proper for a lady to ride a bicycle astride. This debate had been raging since the 1880s with regard to women's horse riding styles and habits (or costumes). The acceptable riding style for women was side saddle and modesty required that she completely cover her legs and ankles with her skirt. Determination to enjoy the freedom of movement offered by the bicycle led to the development of cycling bloomers, an important landmark in freeing women from the restrictions of their clothing.

Aside from its social significance, bicycling was quite possibly the most important sporting activity to affect women's fashion. Once the infamous bloomers had evolved into divided skirts and knickerbocker suits and become acceptable attire, the road was paved for trousers for women. In the 1920s the most fashionable women began to wear trousers for a range of sporting activities including skiing and hiking, while a few of the bravest took to beach pyjamas at the fashionable coastal resorts of Biarritz or

▶ **Ellesse:** 'Guarda' polo shirt.

Monte Carlo. By the time of the Second World War, trousers for women had been given the official seal of approval.

More recently, cycling has again given us a fashion statement. In the late 1970s, cycle messengers in New York adopted the knee-length spandex shorts worn by competitors in the Tour de France. Streetwise stylists and fashion designers soon adapted the look and, dispensing with the padded crotch (indispensable for cushioning on knife-blade thin racing saddles), gave us designer versions that soon became popular as clubwear and streetwear. Even athletes from other sports adopted them: tennis champion André Agassi popularized the wearing of cycle shorts under cotton tennis shorts while many track and field athletes replaced their cottons for thigh-hugging, seemingly aerodynamic spandex.

Major sporting events such as Wimbledon and the Olympic Games have often served as laboratories for technological developments in fabrics and sports apparel design as well as a showcase for fashions. The sporting clothing worn by professional athletes undoubtedly influences the clothing worn by amateurs in the sports and also influences non-sports apparel design.

Contemporary sports stars, who come closest to the western ideal of physical perfection, have also become marketing devices to extend sales of sportswear beyond the professional market to the mass consumer market. A recent survey by Teenage Research Unlimited gave credence to one company's reputation as the leading brand in sports clothing. Out of more than 2000 respondents aged 12 to 19 who were asked to name what they considered to be the coolest brand of any type of product, 42 per cent answered Nike. Nike's advertisements make great use of sports stars endorsing the products, and obviously, to these teenagers, the stars were cool and so, therefore, were Nike's products.

One of the biggest spectator sports in the world is Indy Car racing which has an estimated television audience of more than 75 million in 150 countries. Not surprisingly the fashion industry is keen to climb aboard and this year DKNY Menswear and DK Fragrances are the sponsors of Paul Newman and Carl Haas' Indy Team.

▶ **Penn Sportswear:** moray sweater.

Dresses and skirts

Lawn tennis was one of the first sports to attract widespread interest among women. At first, during the 1870s, they played dressed in long skirts with bustles worn over the mandatory corset, an outfit which did little to encourage free movement around the court. The idea of practical sporting clothes for women did not become a reality until the 1920s when French champion Suzanne Lenglen stepped on to the tennis court without stockings, petticoats and long sleeves in an outfit designed by French *couturier* Jean Patou. Before long, many women had adopted Patou's look of pleated skirt, straight cardigan and short sleeved blouse both for their tenniswear and for casual daywear.

By the 1930s, when fashion dictated a longer skirt length, the practical nature of sports clothes for women was so firmly established that tennis dresses remained short. In the same decade, professional players Alice Marble and Helen Hull Jacobs introduced shorts for women at Wimbledon. In 1949, Teddy Tinling would become a household name, forever associated with the tennis dress of Gussie Moran. 'Gorgeous Gussie' appeared at Wimbledon in a short dress, which, when she raised her arms to serve or return the ball, treated spectators and the world's press to the sight of her matching lace panties. Whatever the style that influences the tennis dress – from Dior's New Look to the mini skirt of the 1960s – one aspect has remained nearly constant: white is the colour.

There are only a few sports in which skirts or dresses continue to be worn for competition – if not for training and practice sessions. In women's hockey, netball and cricket a short, pleated skirt is favoured, a style which no doubt has its origins in British girls' school uniforms.

Ice skating and ice dancing also retain the skirt or dress despite the increasingly complex and athletic range of jumps and spins executed by professionals in the sport. Women skaters continue to wear variations on the outfit made popular back in the

▶ **Lotto:** tennis shirt and 'Huber' skirt in 100 per cent cotton.

1930s by champion skater-turned-Hollywood-star Sonja Henie, precisely because these outfits identify them as women. The age-old gender bias regarding women in sport, though no longer necessarily limiting the range of sports open to women, nevertheless continues to prescribe women's appearance.

Despite the continuing growth in the range of sports open to women competitors both as amateurs and as professionals – the 1996 Atlanta Olympics saw women pole vaulters compete for the first time – and that most women have turned to variations of shorts and trousers for competition, a potential new Olympic sport, competitive ballroom dancing (which appeared at Atlanta as a Demonstration Sport) will mean that the gradual disappearance of dresses and skirts from sport is more than adequately compensated.

◀ **Lacoste:** tenniswear.

▲ **Nike:** 'Mary's dri-fit unidress' with bound scoop neck and armholes, built-in short flared skirt and contrast colour body, skirt and binding.

▼ **Nike:** 'Monica's dress' with short sleeves, scooped front neck, front and back chevron piecing, front lining and a full sweep skirt with turned hem.

Footwear

Despite the often specialist nature of sports footwear, many examples have found their way into everyday use: riding boots, sneakers, basketball shoes and even walking and hiking boots, engineered for the toughest terrains in the world but scaling the streets of cities around the world as part of the Grunge look. Perhaps the most outstanding example of the crossover from specialist sports footwear to mainstream fashion is the running shoe or trainer. We are now so conscious of trainers as designer icons that we even refer to them by their brand names: we put on our Reeboks, Nikes or L.A. Gears.

Born from a hybrid stock of athletic shoes, the trainer spent its youth worn solely by sports people, for sports and with sports apparel. With the fitness craze of the 1970s came the running shoe and a greater number of styles of shoes and boots. To a large extent, however, the emphasis was still on technology and performance. The trainer finally came of age in 1980 when in April a subway strike in New York encouraged thousands of working men and women to walk to work. When the subway strike ended, the trainer stayed put and the trend started for wearing them with tailored suits. Trainers were even mentioned in contemporary literature: protagonist Sherman in *Bonfire of the Vanities* is described as wearing his trainers to work and changing into his Bass Weejuns.

Once the fashion industry had appropriated the technology of the trainer, the shoes gradually became associated with both high fashion and urban youth street style. What both ends of the fashion industry did was to customize the running shoe to suit their own purposes. Urban youths wore their trainers oversize and left the

▶ **Puma:** Puma cell trainer with a contoured sole of interlocking, supple hexagonal cells to improve cushioning, stability and wear. The large cells on the heel and forefoot absorb shock, the more compact cells aid stability.

get
a
life

91 415 7601

change
*the*GAME

FILA

laces undone and dangling on the sidewalks while Karl Lagerfeld put the interlocking initial letters of the founder of the House of Chanel, Coco Chanel, on the most expensive designer versions.

Consequently, today it is possible to buy running shoes for running in – the high-tech specification shoes designed to lessen impact, support the ankle, prevent injury and improve speed and endurance – and running shoes to wear as fashion statements which are manufactured by sports shoe and fashion shoe specialists alike.

While spiked running shoes and soccer boots remain highly specialized footwear in both their design and function, fashion designers have not stopped robbing the sports shoe world for ideas. In 1979 Norma Kamali invented the high-heeled sneaker in the most literal way by cutting away at the top of a black canvas basketball boot and adding a high-stacked rubber heel. More recently, Dirk Bikkenberger produced his designer versions of the golf shoe - complete with rubber studs.

Likewise, sportswear manufacturers are now acutely aware of the need to consider the design of their merchandise beyond the purely functional. The acceptance of a style or brand, particularly by youth subcultures, does much to move large quantities of stock. With the growing popularity of extreme sports such as snowboarding and motorcross and the style of clothing worn by their participants and non-participants, manufacturers like Airwalk, Fila and Underdog are quick to tie their advertising and merchandising of footwear to the concepts of youth, fashion and style.

▲ **Brasher Boots:** lightweight and water resistant boots designed to give maximum grip. Toe and heel are strongly reinforced, the tongue softly padded and pre-shaped and lacing consists of 3D rings and 3-speed hooks.

▲ **Reebok:** 'Hammer' in suede.

▲ **Reebok:** 'Scoundrel' in nubuck.

▲ **Arrow Sports Shoes:** 'Cyclone'
running shoe with window feature in
the outsole.

▼ **Arrow Sports Shoes:** 'Boom' basketball boot with 4 window outsole feature.

▲ **Burton Team Rider,** Dieter Happ
Photo, Ian Mackenzie.

Burton: 'Stumpy' boot: featherweight for freestyle mobility, light and lined, low and flexible.

▼ **Burton:** 'Reactor' boot: 1lb lighter than its competitors.

▼ **adidas.**

▲ **adidas.**

Fila

▼ **Fila:** skateboard shoe.

▲ **Fila:** 'Wheel n Deal'.

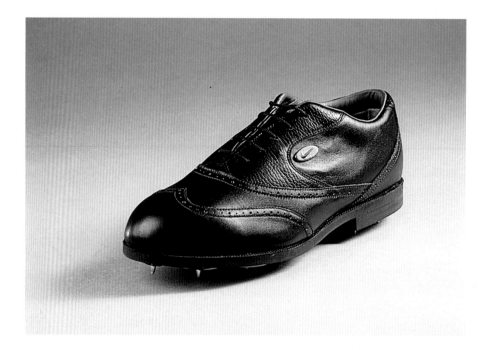

▲ **Nike:** 'Air Zoom Tour Tip' golf shoe with waterproof, breathable full-grain leather upper and Goretex lining. The sole contains a full-length Zoom Air cushioning unit and has green-friendly, long-wearing ceramic spikes.

▶ **Foot-Joy:** Dry Joys waterproof and seam sealed golf shoes. 'IntelliGel' in the sole becomes viscous as it reacts to heat from the foot, leading the sole to conform to the precise shape of the foot's arch.

▲ **Reebok.**

▲ **Reebok.**

▲ **Nike:** 'Tiempo Premier D'
football boot. Lightweight kangaroo
upper; medial and lateral support
straps; inner sleeve and fold over
tongue to enhance fit. Lightweight
Pebax outsole with detachable
aluminium studs; wide heel and a flex
groove in the outer sole.

▼ **Reebok:** 'Instructor Studio pro'.

▼ **Reebok:** 'Aerostep' trainer.

▼ **Fila:** 'Muscleball' basketball shoe.

▼ **Nike:** 'Air Jordan'. Upper of full grain leather and Durabuck with a Phylon wrap ankle support; a full-length midsole and Airsole unit for cushioning, reinforced by a carbon fibre plate.

◀ **adidas.**

▲ **adidas.**

▼ **Nike:** 'Air Max'. Light, synthetic breathable mesh upper with overlay strapping to ensure good fit; sculptured full length midsole for durable cushioning, Airsole lateral crash pad system in heel, separate forefoot air unit, large single flex groove in mid and outersole.

▼ **Converse:** 'Deluge'.

▲ **Converse:** 'All Star Evolution'.

Nike: 'Gabuche' cycling shoe.
Synthetic sole and nylon mesh upper;
2-strap velcro closure system with
additional laces under instep;
premoulded internal heel connector
and toe box for secure fit; lightweight
stiff nylon and glass fill plate for
maximum transfer of energy.

change your liFe

change
*the*GAME

FILA

Headgear

Many items of sports headgear are designed to protect the head from injury: hard riding hats, motor sports crash helmets, fencing masks, Kendo visors and the padded head and face protectors worn by sparring boxers are just a few examples. These are less likely to become fashion accessories than soft-structured hats like baseball caps. Nevertheless, in the growing world of sportswear merchandising, some brands are obviously more desirable and fashionable than others.

The baseball cap has two specific functions within the game: the peak on the front is there to shield the sun from players' eyes and, when worn back to front, the cap allows pitchers and batters movement free from possible obstruction. Today, as well as sporting a team's colours and logo, the baseball cap is associated with a far wider range of sporting and non-sporting activities. Furthermore, it is also the vehicle for many sponsors' names: Formula One racing driver Nigel Mansell's contract with his Japanese sponsor required that he wear a baseball cap bearing the company logo at all times when he gave press and television interviews.

Non-protective sports headgear has two main problems: firstly, it can get in the way and secondly, it can get dislodged in the wind. Close-fitting knitted hats are an obvious solution and, for cyclists who eschew the safety of a helmet, the most fashionable – and one guaranteed to keep your head warm – is a Berber fleece 3-Way hat. This is a soft hat which can be pulled snugly down over the ears, worn with the cuff turned up or worn on top of the head with the crown loose and floppy. The thermal fleece fabric of these hats have made them popular with recreational skiers, snowboarders, skateboarders and winter sports spectators.

Mountain bike speed freaks who would rather keep their brains intact have the ultimate protection in helmets made from a combination of carbon fibre and Kelvar (the material used for bullet proof jackets) with a number of air-vents. Top of the range is the Met Nitro Downhill Helmet which comes complete with a pump-up air bladder to make the helmet fit the head snugly.

▶ **Nordica:** sailor hat worn with insulated jacket and pant.

Glasses and sunglasses are important parts of sports headgear, whether for protection, to aid visibility or just to look good. And one of the main uses of sports headgear is often just to keep the hair out of the eyes of athletes. The towelling sweat bands worn by John McEnroe proved very useful in stopping sweat from getting in his eyes, but such bands do little to control many players' flowing locks. Bandannas seemed to provide a fashionable solution. In America, bandannas had been worn around the necks of cowboys where they could be pulled up over the nose and mouth as a protection against dust. Many an outlaw wore theirs in the same way, but in their case it was to hide their identities. It is this outlaw aspect that most likely led to the popularity of the bandanna with urban street gang members before mainstream fashion took up the style. Bandannas finally appeared on the tennis courts wrapped around the heads of players like Andre Agassi, who sported a pink paisley bandanna at Wimbledon.

◄ **K2:** goggles.

▼ **Oakley:** 'M Frame Heater' sport specific sunglasses for athletes. Plutonite lens material for optical clarity, high-mass and high-velocity impact; ultra light, stress resistant O matter frame material; red iridium lens.

▲ **Oakley:** 'RxM Frame Heater'.

▲ **Oakley:** 'M Frame Heater'.

▲ **Oakley:** 'RX Implants'. Sport
specific sunglasses for athletes with
less than perfect vision. Lens
prescriptions are ground directly on to
the lens of the sunglasses.

◀ **Oakley:** 'M Frame' sport
sunglasses.

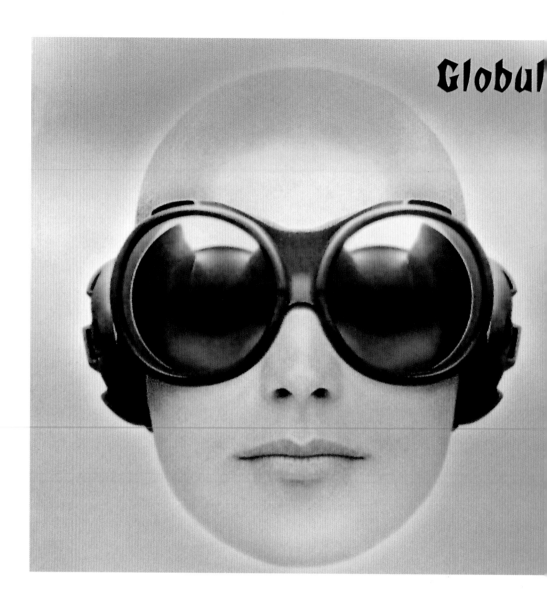

▲ **Bollé:** 'Globule'.

◀ **Bollé:** Attack.

Oakley

▼ **Oakley:** 'Snow Jungle Trenchcoat' with dual spherical lens for a wider peripheral field of vision.

▼ **Oakley:** 'R x Slash' with
vented lens maximizing air flow
to prevent fogging.

▼ **Oakley:** 'Slash' iridium lens.

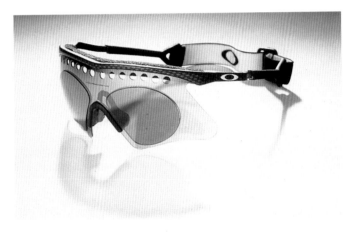

▶ **Lotto:** baseball cap and polar fleece top.

▲ **Oakley:** 'Zero 0.6' glasses reduce distortion at all angles of vision; earsocks and nose pieces become more adhesive as the wearer sweats, thus maintaining a secure fit.

Jackets

The words 'sports jacket' conjure up an image of a conventionally tailored man's jacket made in tweed, checked or plain woollen fabric, a garment that is only a little less formal than its brother the suit jacket. This notion dates back to the eighteenth century. In *Modesty in Dress: An Enquiry into the Fundamentals of Fashion* (1969) costume and fashion historian James Laver suggests that all modern forms of men's dress originate in sportswear. Everyday riding clothes – the sporting dress – made of wool in the muted colours of the countryside and worn by the landed gentry of the eighteenth century evolved into the suits worn by nineteenth-century city men, replacing the fine laces, satins and velvets that had once been essential to the fashionable man-about-town.

The riding jacket remains a mainstay, not just for equestrian athletes but also for fashion designers and manufacturers of classic clothing, ranging from long-established companies like Burberry, Austin Reed and Aquascutum to contemporary designers Margaret Howell and Ralph Lauren.

The crossover of contemporary sportswear jackets to mainstream fashion is mainly confined to fabric technology. Many of today's fashion designers have incorporated thermal fabrics into their collections like Polar Fleece, a soft, fleecy fabric originally used in the manufacture of climbing, walking and camping survival wear, and Gore-Tex, a fabric which breathes and keeps the wearer's skin dry in wet conditions. Jackets specifically designed for sports have made the transition to fashion icon, amongst them Puffa quilted ski jackets, hooded zip-front sweatshirt jackets and baseball jackets. The most obvious example remains the leather biker's jacket. Once purely functional – it was windproof, supple enough to allow the rider to move yet sufficiently strong to protect him from injury should he fall – now numerous variations turn up each season on the catwalks of Milan and Paris while its country cousin in blue denim or cotton drill remains equally popular.

▶ **Nordica:** insulated jacket with Japanese logo and basic insulated pant.

Today, companies like Serious, Cybertek and Avirex, manufacturers of extreme sports clothing, have responded to their customers' demands for garments that combine functionality with high-tech fabric innovations and performance with style and now produce highly covetable collections.

◀ **Proquip:** 2-layer golf suit with blouson style jacket. The outer layer is of waterproof, windproof and breathable Goretex.

▼ **Le Coq Sportif:** (Right) 'San
Paolo' drill top in sueded cotton drill.
(Left) 'Inter' rain jacket in nylon rip
stop with polyester mesh lining and
taping overlay on shoulder and sleeves.

▼ **Le Coq Sportif:** 'Madison' zip
fronted hooded top with lined check
hood contrast and stitch detail.

▼ **Chevignon:** reversible
goose down jacket.

▶ **Chevignon:** 'All European' goose down
jacket. Photo Thiemo Sander

◀ **Malins:** Etaproof fishing jacket. Etapoof is a versatile performance fabric: durable and water repellant.

▲ **Fred Perry:** nylon sports jacket.
Mesh lining; cord side-adjusters; polar
fleece collar lining; zip pockets;
eyelets; velcro-adjustable cuffs.

▼ **Burton:** 'Tri-Lite Convertible Jacket'. 3-ply Tri-Lite shell for maximum protection; taped seams; front zipper with low tack velcro storm flap; contour hood and slash drawcord at waist and hem.

▶ **Burton Team Rider**, Jason Brown
Photo, Jeff Curtes

▼ **Nike:** 'TW streak' packable jacket
and matching pants. O-ring zipper pull;
inner storm fly; vented zip pockets;
nylon/elastane binding at collar and
cuffs; shock cord drawstring waist with
toggle closure each side; reflective
piping and stash pocket in lower back
that converts into a bum bag.

▶ **K2:** ski jacket with matching pants.

▲ **Burton:** 'Outland' waterproof convertible jacket with removable contour hood; front zipper with velcro storm flap; microfibre lined collar; neck warmer fleece panel; articulated elbows and venting zips at armpits.

▼ **Burton Team Rider**,
Nicolas Conte Photo, Jeff Curtes

Shirts

Some shirts worn for sports remain formal and very close in style to dress shirts: equestrian shirts have a loop on the outside seam of the collar through which the stock (the tie) is passed. Other sports shirts like the three-button polo shirt, the tennis shirt, the soccer shirt and of course, the tee-shirt are today also worn away from the gym and the sports field. The ultimate in designer polo shirts has to be one that carries the Ralph Lauren Polo logo: the fashion designer has managed to appropriate the generic name of the shirt and transform it into a brand name.

Close in style to the polo shirt is the tennis shirt. Prior to 1926, gentlemen tennis players – both amateurs and professionals – stepped on to the court in long-sleeved shirts with stiff collars and a necktie. In this year, the French champion René Lacoste designed the tennis shirt that would be forever associated with the sport and, in the 1980s, would become the shirt most favoured by some soccer fans: the Lacoste short-sleeve tennis shirt in cotton pique. Because of his aggression on the court, Lacoste had been nicknamed Le Crocodile and he devised a crocodile logo which he emblazoned across his shirt. In 1933 Lacoste's shirt went into production and since then, has retained both the logo and, in America, one original design feature – the long tail which means that the shirt stays firmly tucked in the waistband of shorts during play. It is estimated that more than 200 million Lacoste shirts have been sold worldwide and it is so popular a brand that, in the designer name frenzy of the 1990s, it is probably the most copied and counterfeited article of sportswear ever.

The only shirt likely to have outsold the Lacoste tennis shirt is the humble tee-shirt. Despite being a mainstay of both our sporting and fashion wardrobe, it in fact started life as underwear for soldiers during the First World War and was later worn as workwear. So versatile is this simple garment that it carries political slogans, designer

▲ **Lacoste:** polo shirts.

logos, team names, national flags, offensive messages and even holograms. Nocturnal joggers can now enjoy the benefit of tee-shirts with Glo-Works, a battery operated material based on the technology of Air Force emergency landing strips. The material, which can be made extremely thin, can also be bent and twisted and, when lit up, is visible up to a quarter of a mile away.

One recent cross-over from sports clothing to street style has been the soccer shirt. The style – and the fabrics – has been adopted by many designers and manufacturers like X-Dreem to produce fashionable versions aimed specifically at the youth market. But the most loyal fans will, no doubt, still wear their team's colours both as a mark of loyalty to the club and also as a way of signalling their attachment to a particular town, city or even nation. So popular are soccer shirts with fans as leisurewear that in addition to being sold through sports shops, most soccer clubs now have their own retail outlets. Nevertheless, clubs severely test the loyalty of many of its fans (if not their parents) when they decide to introduce entirely new sets of home and away strips.

◄ **Fila:** polo shirt.

▼ **Prince.**

▶ **Prince:** 'Optical' collarless shirt in stretch rib fabric.

◀ **Fila:** basketball singlet.

▲ **Nike:** 'Dri fit' racing singlet with matching shorts. Colour blocked with a partial front lining; slightly curved hem and self fabric binding at neck and armholes.

▼ **Prince:** tennis shirt with collar and centre front zip.

▲ **Lacoste:** tennis shirt.

▼ **Helly Hansen:** 'Lifa Bodywear'
long-sleeved vest from polypropylene.

◀ **Star Sportswear:** football shirt.

▼ **USA Pro:** 'Sportica' v-necked top in cotton Lycra with logo elastic highlighting waistband and side seams.

◀ **USA Pro:** 'Cyberspace' v-necked cropped top in sueded cotton lycra with reflective tape straps.

Suits

The term suit, when applied to sports apparel, can mean either a two-piece outfit — a tracksuit or shellsuit — or a one-piece outfit like a catsuit or swimsuit. Some sports retain their traditional styles — judo and dressage are examples — while others have changed as the sport has evolved.

Technically, tracksuits and shellsuits are sporting accessories since they are not usually worn beyond the warm-up stage or the cool-down period — except of course when they are worn as fashionable casualwear!

Both tracksuits and shellsuits have, at some time, found their way into the fashion wardrobes of men and women of all ages (and sporting abilities) and Paul Smith, Katharine Hamnett, Calvin Klein, Donna Karan and Giorgio Armani have included and continue to include their versions of sweat tops and pants in their ready-to-wear collections. While sweatshirting fabrics and thermal fabrics like Polar Fleece remain popular choices, the lightweight shiny fabric shellsuit has become a fashion don't and an object of derision even on the sports field.

A growing number of track and field sportsmen and women have adopted the all-in-one spandex catsuit — either legless, like a swimsuit, or with legs — as wind resistance is reduced and loosely-fitting clothing may interfere with sports' equipment. In the 1988 Summer Olympics at Seoul, South Korea, Florence Griffith-Joyner (known to fans and sportscasters alike as Flo-Jo) made headlines not only with her world record-breaking sprinting but also with her fashion statements which included one-legged and hooded catsuits and long, colourfully-painted fingernails.

The racing swimsuit has also filtered into fashion in both its style and its fabric technology. In 1973 the East German women's Olympic swimming team cast off their old-style nylon swimsuits for second skin resistance-free spandex suits and took seconds off Olympic records.

▶ **Converse Active:** 'Allstar Ladies' hooded track top from nylon interlock; legging in lycra jersey with piping and contrast trim on neckline and sleeves.

Novelty features added to synthetic fibres to make them 'intelligent' now allow fabrics to change colour. Some fabrics appear white at temperatures of 23°C and above but turn to vivid colours when below 14°C. DuPont is set to launch a new quality Lycra, Type 269B, which has greater properties of stretch and recovery. Furthermore, it has a higher resistance to chlorine and, whether you wear a regulation swimsuit or a fashion swimsuit, the colour will not fade as quickly.

The latest concept in fashion swimwear is the Sun-Select range of tan-through fabrics. The latest fabric, called JS006, is a blend of 82 per cent Sun-Select high-tech polyester and 18 per cent DuPont Lycra, which allows the skin beneath the fabric to be tanned but also protects the body against the harmful effects of UV radiation.

◀ **K2:** skiwear.

▼ **Sola:** 'Evolution' wetsuit from 3mm Neoprene; double lined lower body for durability; Finemesh and Supercomposite Skin supple upper body; contrast flatlocked, stitched and heat taped seams.

▶ **The Shark Group:** 'Interaction' wetsuits for waterskiing and windsurfing.

◀ **Rasurel:** one-piece swimsuit.

▲ **Speedo:** 'Sonic Tank' beach
volleyball suit.

▼ **Lotto:** lycra leotard.

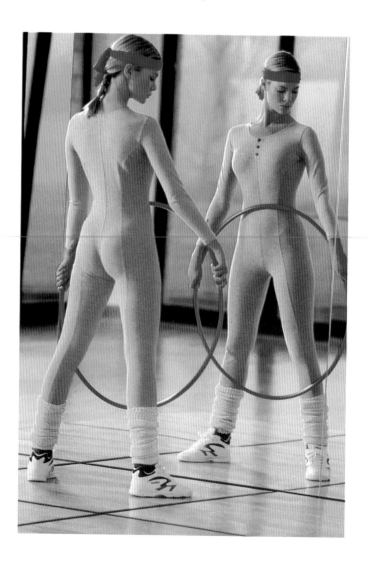

▲ **USA Pro:** 'Sportica' uni.

▼ **Lotto:** 'Boris' microfibre tracksuit.

▼ **Star Sportswear:** tracksuit.

▶ **K2:** skiwear.
▼

Sweaters

The sweater, as its name implies, was first worn to encourage sweating. Only a few sports, like cricket and golf, still retain the original woollen sweater as part of their sporting dress. Although a summer game, cricket can be notoriously slow and the British summer predictably cold and the woollen sweater with its V-neck is a necessary item for outfielders. Some players opt for sleeveless versions which allow for a freer movement of the arms. For golfers, the need is similarly for body warmth coupled with freedom of movement. V-necked sweaters for women were not worn until just before the First World War as the neckline was thought immodest.

Where once sweaters in the fashion world meant casual dressing, knitwear today can be perceived as being almost as formal as suits, particularly as new fabrics have replaced wool in sports apparel – fabrics which either help demonstrate and display our sweat (the all important indicator of a body working out) or lighter weight fabrics which absorb sweat more effectively, thereby keeping the body dry and warm.

The golf sweater has entered the vocabulary of fashion dressing, whether we play the game or simply watch it from the clubhouse or armchair. Most knitwear departments of fashion stores offer a range of colours and makes, including brands bearing the names of famous pros like Jack Nicklaus. The traditional brightly-patterned woollen ski-jumper has also gone the same fashion route. New technology has largely replaced the need for woollen winter sports clothing with the development of less itchy, lighter and faster drying fabrics. Probably the most important development in fabric technology of the 1980s and 1990s has been that of microfibres, originally polyester fibres that were finer than human hair or were even pure silk filaments. ICI Fibres were the first with Tactel in the early 1980s but by the end of the decade the original simple fibres had been expanded into a whole range of yarns including Tactel Micro, specifically engineered for active sportswear. Now a whole host of companies

▶ **Ellesse:** classic sweatshirt in ocean.

▲ **Fila:** knitwear.
◀

have registered their microfibre brand names like Diolen Micro, Zero 4, Setila and Micromattique. When microfibres are densely woven, they provide a good degree of water repellency, yet for real waterproofing a special finish is still required. One of the finest filament yarns produced is Terital Zero 4. So tightly woven that it can be used for tents for Arctic explorers, it has also replaced the traditional oilskins used by racing yachtsmen. With this fabric, the body's water vapour and perspiration can pass from the skin out through the fibre filaments, yet raindrops and melted snowflakes can not enter. And because the fabric is windproof, it is ideal for downhill ski runs!

In recent years Japanese manufacturers have added novelty features to their fibres, now called 'intelligent'. While fashion designers may have picked up on the gimmicky nature of some of these new fibres – those which change colour according to body temperature, perfumed fibres activated by body movements and even fabric which contains vitamins – when applied to active sports clothing these fibres can, in fact, serve very useful functions. The addition of inorganic carbon particles to the fibres helps to keep the body warm by converting infrared radiation from sunlight into thermal energy: a possibly life-saving function for which any skier or snowboarder lost on the mountainside would be grateful.

◀ **Lotto:** fleece sweatshirt in 100 per cent cotton.

Ellesse

◀ **Ellesse:** 'Mailborne' sweatshirt and
▼ (below) classic male sweatshirt.

Trousers and shorts

Many trousers originally worn as sportswear have found their way into the wardrobe of fashion: jodhpurs, motorcyclist's leather trousers, cycling shorts and ski pants have all made their appearance on the catwalks and in the high street.

After the Second World War, when new synthetic fabrics became widely available, tapered ankle-length pants, secured at the instep by an elastic strap or stirrup, became the style on the slopes. This figure-hugging style remains popular both on the high street and on the mountainside but there are differences. The term ski pants is now the generic name for the fashion garment while, on the slopes, down-hill racers have largely adopted body hugging spandex all-in-one catsuits to cut down wind resistance and save vital nano-seconds.

With the increased interest in extreme sports like off-piste skiing and snowboarding, speed is somewhat less important than mobility and survival. Single-layer figure-hugging garments like ski pants are totally unsuited to these sports where windproofing, snowproofing, waterproofing and thermal insulation are necessities. Loosely fitting pants in fabrics like Gore-Tex and Activent are needed for performing snowboarding stunts and for staying alive on multi-day ski treks.

In men's gymnastics, a similar style of pants to the ski pant with stirrup ankle is worn. Its style betrays the sport's military academy origin: they are similar in style to nineteenth-century cavalry officer's breeches and the sport today continues to include displays of agility on the horse.

Most track and field sports – with the exception of cricket, the equestrian sports and golf – have turned from trousers to shorts for their sporting attire. Surprisingly, in tennis, where shorts are often seen as the uniform, it was men's modesty that stopped them from wearing shorts until British champion Bunny Austin took the daring

▶ **Marika:** 'Power Thin-Her' tights for aerobicwear.

decision to step onto the court at Forest Hills in 1932 in what the newspapers variously described as Air-Cooled Trousers and Ventilated Pants. Austin, in his book *Lawn Tennis Made Easy*, describes his torment over the decision to play in shorts rather than longs and how the doorman at his hotel whispered to him that he had forgotten to put his trousers on!

Today, shorts – whether baggy cotton soccer style, knee-length and baggy cut-offs in sweatshirting or spandex cycle shorts – are all worn for non-sporting activities. We await the day when the satin shorts and dressing gowns of boxers become streetwear. Meanwhile, *GQ* in its *Active* supplement for Winter 1996, gives advice on 'How to look cool on a bike: real cyclists don't wear spandex shorts any more! This autumn's look is retro with Tudor Tights – all black leggings with a fleecy woollen lining and multi coloured world championship ribbing at the ankles.' You need to wear braces to keep them up, but *GQ* predicts that they will be the thing to wear with a Comme des Garçons suit!

◀ **Fila:** baseball shorts and matching singlet.

Lotto: 'Becker' junior tennis shirt
and shorts.
'Muster' junior tennis shirt and shorts.

▼

▼ **Burton:** 'Tri-Lite' pant. 3 ply Tri-Lite shell with taped seams; hip to knee zipper; side vents with dual storm vents; gathered back warmer panel; Duawear cuffs; kickpatch panels and interior gaiters.

▲ Burton Team Rider, Christine
Rauter Photo Ian Mackenzie

▼ Burton Team Rider, Peter Bauer
Photo, Richard Walch

▶ **Nordica:** basic insulated pant with
lightbulb insulated pull-on cap.

Index

▶ **Ellesse**: 'Augusta' sport dress in white.

Index